THE MOUNTAIN OF GOD

BRINGING FREEDOM TO SATANICALLY DEPRESSED AREAS

PARRIS PATRICK

CLAY BRIDGES
PRESS

The Mountain of God
Bringing Freedom to Satanically Depressed Areas

Published by Clay Bridges in Houston, TX
www.claybridgespress.com

ISBN 978-1-953300-84-3 (paperback)
ISBN 978-1-953300-83-6 (ebook)

Special Sales: Most Clay Bridges titles are available in special quantity discounts. Custom imprinting or excerpting can also be done to fit special needs. For standard bulk orders, go to www.claybridgesbulk.com. For specialty press or large orders, contact Clay Bridges at info@claybridgespress.com.

This book is dedicated to all who see the forces of darkness having an impact on your community and who are searching for what God is doing. I pray this book in some way serves to answer your questions and guide you into what God would have you do to bring His light and disperse the darkness!

TABLE OF CONTENTS

SPECIAL THANKS

I would like to thank the many kingdom brothers and sisters who served as sounding boards and kind critics while this work was being birthed. I would like to specifically thank Pastor Kevin Riser of South Belt Church and John Butler. Words cannot express how your love and just "being there" during this process impacted me. You both raised my arms when I was too tired to hold them up and wanted to give up: thank you.

INTRODUCTION

A "satanically depressed area" can be described as one where a region or territory is occupied by fallen angels without much contention by forces of light. The goal is to control an entire region and not specifically the people within it.

Control over the region will give automatic control over the people. A brief study into war tactics reveals that, if an invading military's goal is to control a region, they will not attack the people first. They will attack the city, cutting off supply lines, destroying access points into and out of the city, and disrupting city infrastructure and government—all with the goal of controlling the city **and** its inhabitants. They are not seeking the city's destruction—

just its strategic value. We can see this in the war tactics used during World War II.

So, as it is manifested in the natural, it is also done in the spiritual.

Every city, every community has strategic value to God, but the same can also be said about how Satan values a city. Consider the words in Ephesians 6:12:

> *For our struggle is not against flesh and blood, but against the rulers, against the authorities, against the cosmic powers of this darkness, against evil, spiritual forces in the heavens.*

To see this warfare, you've got to be able to see beyond what you are seeing in the people and begin looking for the unseen "rulers of darkness" in your community.

The goal of this book is to share with you my journey of having my eyes opened to what is happening in my community. My prayer is that you will ask God to open your eyes to what He wants done in your community; then God will give you a strategy to stop what Satan is doing.

When the servant of the man of God got up and went out early the next morning, an army with horses and chariots had surrounded the city. "Oh no, my lord! What shall we do?" the servant asked. "Don't be afraid," the prophet answered. "Those who are with us are more than those who are with them." And Elisha prayed, "Open his eyes, LORD, so that he may see." Then the LORD opened the servant's eyes, and he looked and saw the hills full of horses and chariots of fire all around Elisha.

—2 Kings 6:15–17 NIV

HOW THIS BEGAN

I minister in a community called Alief; it's a multicultural melting pot representing almost every nation and people group on the planet. I also grew up in Alief—I was not born there but arrived as soon as I could! When I was growing up in Alief, seventh grade through high school graduation, it was like almost every middle-class community in America. There were problems in Alief like in any community, but there was also a very strong presence of God-fearing, Bible-teaching churches to combat the presence of evil that tries to overtake every community.

I left Alief in 1996 to attend college and seminary, then got married in 1999 and moved my family to Missouri City, Texas. About 2008, my wife and I began to feel a very strong pull from God to plant a church. Not just any church. A church in Alief. I felt good about this because when I left Alief, churches were strong, growing, and winning souls every Sunday.

When my wife, Chantell, and I drove through Alief in 2009 to see where God wanted us to plant the church He had so clearly placed in our hearts, we were surprised by what we saw. Alief had become a literal graveyard of churches that had closed their doors or sold their property to other religious groups. Those religions moved into the area and held celebrations as they removed crosses off the buildings they had purchased—church buildings that just a few years before had been centers of gospel light. Many of the churches that remained were either struggling to survive or had succumbed to the "itching ear teaching" Paul warned about in 2 Timothy 4:3. The number of God-fearing, Bible-teaching churches had dwindled to just a few.

As we drove around and surveyed the community, we could see that certain areas were worse than others. Some areas were dealing with horrible cases of racism; others were living in harmony; still other areas became known for prostitution and drugs, while some areas were dealing with gang activity or petty crimes. Without knowing it, we had stumbled upon the divisive tactics of our enemy as he operates in invisible wicked high places, and it was destroying the very community where God asked us to plant our church.

We were very confused. I began to question my calling to Alief. Many thoughts began to flood in: "Perhaps God simply wanted me to plant a church anywhere." "Maybe the location did not matter." "Maybe God was calling me to an existing church that was looking for a pastor." Nothing I did or tried stopped or quieted the pull that we felt from God to plant a church in Alief. So, in June 2009, we planted and launched our church in Alief.

At first, everything seemed okay; we outgrew our living room and moved to a school, then we needed to move out of the school and found a small storefront to rent. It was in this storefront that I had my first encounter with God revealing to me the invisible battle that had so affected His church body.

PART 1
THEN THE DREAMS CAME

Dream 1

In the first of what would be many dreams to come, God revealed to me that He wanted me to cause "His people" to fall back in love with Him so that they would continue the work he sent them to do with faith and fervor.

As I reflected on this dream and asked God for more input and insight, I began to focus on the fact that He had asked me to focus on "His People." Not unsaved people, not people who had never heard the gospel, but "His people." It was the first time I began to realize that the problems in my community, in Alief, were not solely being caused by people who were unbelieving and far from God, but by believers, His children, "His people" who had chosen, for whatever reason, to live away from the church and contrary to the truth. I started asking myself, "What happened to the condition of the church between 1996, when I left, and 2009, when I came back?" Everything God would reveal to me after this was in response to that question.

Shortly after this dream, we moved to a new location, deeper into Alief and much closer to what could be considered the middle of the community. Despite many community outreach drives and servant evangelism events, we saw little return. I decided to poll the community and ask why they were not coming to church. We asked three main questions:

1. Are you a Christian?
2. Do you have a church home?
3. Do you attend church regularly? If not, why not?

Then we asked if we could pray for them and/or their household.

We knocked on over 2,000 doors and what we found out was that well over 80% of those polled were believers in Jesus Christ; however, they no longer attended church due to something that had happened to them or to someone they knew. Most of the time, the offending party was in church leadership; there were even a few accounts of the pastor himself being the offender. We started matching up the years of all the reported offenses, and they matched up perfectly: 1996 to 2009. So, I was right, something did happen to Alief during the years I was gone: the darkness had grown because the centers of gospel light had dimmed. I asked the Lord what He wanted me to do with all this information; I knew it could not be for nothing.

At this point, here were the facts I knew:

1. God called me to cause His people, His church, to fall back in love with Him so that they would continue the work He sent them to do with faith and fervor.
2. Something had happened to the church in Alief between the years of 1996 and 2009, causing the people to fall out of love with God and, hence, stop the work He sent them to do.
3. I knew there was more God wanted to show me about the church-graveyard that was Alief.

Then Came My "Boardroom Dreams" 2, 3, 4, and 5

I can only describe these dreams as "personal experiences in which I did not know whether I was dreaming or actually seeing or hearing something that was occurring."

In other words, while I am recounting this as a dream, in reality, what I truly am describing to you is something that I physically experienced that I cannot describe to you in any other words than to just simply say, "I was there." After I've recounted all four dreams, I'll share with you what God revealed to me.

Boardroom Dream 2

During a season of fasting and prayer, I began to study Isaiah 58 and the fast that God had chosen while also spending a lot of time studying the works of Henry Blackaby and his series called *Experiencing God.* My goal was to get a strategy from God on what He wanted me to do in the community He sent me to. Close to the end of the fast, God allowed me to be in a boardroom in which Satan was meeting with his fallen angels. In this meeting, the first thing I wondered was, "Why can't they see me?" Then I realized that this meeting was about me.

Present at this meeting were the demons assigned to my wife and children, the demons of busyness and distraction, and a few other demons assigned to keep me discouraged. Satan was present also. They were like normal people, well-dressed and well-spoken. They were meeting about, and I quote, "He (referring to me) has figured out how to tap into the power of God; we must keep him (referring to me again) distracted and discouraged or we (speaking of themselves) will lose ground." Satan was instructing the demon assigned to my wife on how to irritate her and get to me; then he (Satan) was instructing the demons assigned to my children to hurt the father-child bond I shared with my children, so that my attention would turn to my kids. He instructed the demons of busyness and distraction to make me busy, but not effective and discouraged with only glimpses of comfort. Then it occurred to me, all the things happening in my life had been strategically and methodically planned and were being executed with precision and purpose. Satan never once lost his temper, and he spoke with an even tone. It was obvious he was in control of the room; although, I did sense his worry that somehow I had stumbled into tapping into God's power on earth. I could hardly believe that God had hidden my presence in this room. The things I heard and saw never would have been revealed if they knew I was there. Upon waking from this dream-vision, I knew that what I had experienced was beyond a dream, it was . . . something else, and it wasn't the last.

Boardroom Dream 3

Shortly after the first boardroom dream while continuing to study Blackaby's *Experiencing God*, God allowed me to attend another boardroom meeting with Satan and his demons. This time, they were discussing how to keep single mothers from trusting relationships with men. In this room Satan was speaking to a select number of demons; I don't know the exact number, but it was not more than twenty. For the duration of his speech, addressing the entire room, there were times when he only spoke directly to the demons of entitlement, laziness (slothfulness), independence, and rebellion.

To the demon of entitlement, he said: "*Keep them (referring to single mothers) thinking that they deserve and are owed money and houses. Make them become angry if anyone attempts to lessen the amount of resources they feel like they are entitled to.*"

To the demon of laziness (slothfulness), he said: "*Make sure they are always aware of the minimum requirements of their entitlement.*"

To the demons of independence and rebellion, he said: "*When the fathers of the children want to come back, make sure they (the mothers) are fully aware that if the man comes home, they will lose their resources. Cause them to feel that as long as they have their resources, they don't need a man in the house and that they can fill the role of mother and father themselves.*"

I don't remember the rest of what he said in detail, only that he (Satan) was very concerned that the men were beginning to want to come and fill their roles as fathers, and that caused him much concern.

Boardroom Dream 4

During another time of fasting and prayer, I began studying the books of Ezra and Nehemiah. I was unpacking the revival that occurred in Ezra chapters 8–10. Again, I found myself in a boardroom meeting with Satan and his demons. God had hidden my presence from them again, as he had so many times before. Present at this meeting were the demon over the school district, the demon over the prison system, Satan, and other demons. I was not aware of why they were in the room. They were discussing the success of their oppression over the Alief community and whether to leave and move elsewhere or to stay. It was interesting because Satan did not run this meeting like the others; instead, he was seeking the opinion of the other demons who were present. Once Satan asked the opening question, he did not speak. I was not able to hear all the conversations taking place in the room; however, toward the end of the meeting, the demon over the prison system stood and said loudly, "We cannot leave this area because there is still too much money here to be made." Shortly after that, I awoke.

As I reflected on this dream-vision, all I could think was, "What do demons want with money?" "What was money to them?"

Boardroom Dream 5

This dream did not occur in a boardroom, but I include it with the boardroom dreams because it happened in the same short span of time as the boardroom dreams.

I was studying 2 Chronicles chapter 14 and the healing of the land based on the repentance and healing of God's people. In this dream I was somehow being carried far from Alief. Once I was a good distance away, I was turned around and was able to see Alief from very far and very high. What I saw was amazing and startling. There was a dragon breathing fire over the entire Alief community. The fire was constant and intense; the dragon never once stopped to take a breath, and the sweeping of its head was on a consistent, timed pattern. I never saw who or what was carrying me, but I knew I was safe and protected. The longer I looked at the flames coming out of the dragon, the more I began to recognize that there was something in the flames. Then, almost instantly, I was within a few feet of the dragon. At this close proximity, I was able to see that the flames were not flames at all but words. The dragon was spewing out flaming words of oppression. Here are the words I was able to remember once I woke from this vision: hate, racism, sex, depression, anger, loneliness, drugs, poverty, money, despair, and envy. There were so many words, and the stream of them was constant, repeating and unending.

When I woke, it was clear to me that God was beginning to show me that there was demonic and spiritual oppression over Alief that was manifesting itself in the actions of the population of the community. Truly the ruler of darkness was attempting to claim this area.

Reflections

PART 2
WHAT THESE DREAMS REVEALED

How God Used My Boardroom Dreams

These dream-visions occurred over the span of almost two years. While I have dreams quite often, these five dream-visions are what I believe God used to answer my initial question: "What happened to the church (and as a result, the community) in Alief between 1996 and 2009?"

Up to this point in my journey, here is what I knew:

1. God called me to cause His people, His church, to fall back in love with Him so that they would continue the work he sent them to do, with faith and fervor.

2. Something had happened to the church in Alief between the years of 1996 and 2009, causing the people to fall out of love with God and, hence, stop the work He sent them to do.
3. I knew there was more God wanted to show me about the church-graveyard that was Alief.

Because of my experience of the boardroom dream-visions, I was able add the following to what I knew:

1. There was a strategy against my life to keep me from continuing to learn how to attract God's presence to Alief and help bring revival. I began to realize that busyness, letdowns, betrayals, sudden lack of provision, my suicidal thoughts, and even my marriage separation and possible divorce—all were from Satan and his demons to make me quit or to divert me into handling never-ending emergencies.
2. Satan values Alief, and there is something in Alief that he considers "money."
3. Nothing was just happening; Satan's strategies and war tactics were planned and well-thought-out. Satan had managed to outthink and out-implement the local churches through the unity of his board meetings.

4. Satan wanted to make sure the men stayed away, or if they came back, they were not to be seen as having any authority in their families or our community.
5. There was an attack on single mothers to make them dependent on a system, rather than being dependent on God.
6. Satan had somehow infiltrated the school system and prison system. Whatever Satan considered "money" was being made through the partnership of the schools and prisons. Somehow, Satan had ambassadors of darkness implanted in these institutions, and they were helping to keep Alief under oppression.
7. I learned from the dragon-dream that Satan was blinding the minds of the people in the community by bombarding all of Alief with the works of the flesh. Everything Alief saw, heard, and experienced was connected to the words coming out of that dragon's mouth. Truly evil communications were corrupting good morals (1 Cor. 15:33).

How Did It Get This Bad?

It was obvious now that God was showing me that Alief had fallen far from Him and that His blessings and protections had diminished. This in turn allowed for great oppression and bondage in the community. As I reflected on my dream of the dragon and what it was spewing from its mouth in the flames, I began to study Ezekiel and the things that God showed him that led to the destruction of Jerusalem. The similarities were surprising.

Ezekiel 8:3–6

> *He stretched out what appeared to be a hand and took me by the hair of my head. Then the Spirit lifted me up between earth and heaven and carried me in visions of God to Jerusalem, to the entrance of the inner gate that faces north, where the offensive statue that provokes jealousy was located. I saw the glory of the God of Israel there, like the vision I had seen in the plain. The* Lord *said to me, "Son of man, look toward the north." I looked to the north, and there was this offensive statue north of the Altar Gate, at the entrance. He said to me, "Son of man, do you see what they are doing*

> *here—more detestable acts that the house of Israel is committing—so that I must depart from my sanctuary? You will see even more detestable acts."*

This is the beginning of Ezekiel's journey with God as He shows Ezekiel why He is about to lift His presence from the temple and eventually from Israel altogether. This would in fact be the last time that the physical presence of God Himself dwelled with mankind. In the church age, God's presence dwells on the earth within His temple, which is the physical bodies of the Church—we believers collectively (1 Cor. 6:19).

Ezekiel's vision-journey is a progression of images and activities that are offensive to God, that go from bad to worse. In this first instance, as Ezekiel is being carried around by a lock of his hair, he is taken to a location in Jerusalem called the inner gate, facing north. There he sees two things: first, the Glory of God and second, an "Image of Jealousy," which is an idol of some kind that was set up next to the presence of God. It was causing God to be provoked to jealousy.

God expresses His displeasure in the fact that this idol worship was not only being committed by the people but also by the priests in the temple. It was so bad in the temple that God could not rest His presence in His sanctuary (Ezek. 8:6)! He ends this episode by telling Ezekiel that He has something even worse to show him.

Correlation to Alief

If you take a tour of Alief, you will find statues of idols everywhere. In fact, the tallest idol in Houston is in Alief. These idols began showing up in droves between 1996 and 2009. What is most interesting however is the number of churches that sold their buildings and properties during these years to idol-worshipping religions. They sold not to other churches to sustain the gospel presence of God, but to other religions who would bring in idols and much worse. The reason the churches sold their property is not nearly as important as realizing that in the act of selling to idol-worshipping religions, a source of God's presence was lifted from Alief—a candle was removed from its candlestick. Was money an idol? Did they praise God for the money they received upon selling their properties that allowed idols in? In selling to these "idol worshippers," did they pass over other gospel-centered churches that perhaps could not offer as much money? No matter how you answer these questions, the fact remains . . . the body of Christ in Alief gave up territory to the enemy, for money. That, in my book, makes this an idol and is another reason, in a long list of other reasons, why God's influence in Alief was weakened.

Ezekiel 8:7–13

> *Then he brought me to the entrance of the court, and when I looked there was a hole in the wall. He said to me, "Son of man, dig through the wall." So I dug through the wall and discovered a doorway. He said to me, "Go in and see the detestable, wicked acts they are committing here." I went in and looked, and there engraved all around the wall was every kind of abhorrent thing—crawling creatures and beasts—as well as all the idols of the house of Israel. Seventy elders from the house of Israel were standing before them, with Jaazaniah son of Shaphan standing among them. Each had a firepan in his hand, and a fragrant cloud of incense was rising up. He said to me, "Son of man, do you see*

> *what the elders of the house of Israel are doing in the darkness, each at the shrine of his idol? For they are saying, 'The* Lord *does not see us. The* Lord *has abandoned the land.'" Again he said to me, "You will see even more detestable acts that they are committing."*

This passage describes the second location, the door of the court, that God has taken Ezekiel to see. At this location God shows Ezekiel the private lives of the people and of the elders. The elders, while not priests, were important in the function of worshipping God and in the spiritual health of Israel (see Exod. 24:1). Today, we could equate these people to deacons, elders, or pastors in most Protestant churches.

Publicly they were for God; but privately they worshipped every form of creeping thing and idols. It's very reminiscent of the description of people in Romans 1, who the Lord gave over to a reprobate mind. They concluded that God could not see what they did in hiding. (They did not understand the longsuffering of God that does not punish right away but instead gives us time to repent.) It's interesting that in Ezekiel 8:12, God is especially offended by what the elders were doing. Even with all of this being done by the elders, God tells Ezekiel that there is still worse coming.

Correlation to Alief

During our house-to-house interviews when we were investigating what happened to the *churches* in Alief between 1996 and 2009, we learned that many of the offenses that caused people to flee their church came from people in church leadership. We have written documentation of people's money being taken in school loan fraud and insurance fraud; church leaders having affairs with the spouses of their members; and leaders being caught in prostitution stings. We've seen copies of text messages and cell phone pictures as evidence of the secret activities of many church leaders. This is proof positive that there is a separation between what many church leaders purported themselves to be in public between 1996 and 2009 and who they were in private. It is important to note here that it is not my intention to further hurt the reputation of the church; I'm simply stating the correlation between what God showed Ezekiel and what God has shown me in my research into the health of the local church in my community. It is also important to note that while it is clear there is a problem in the health of the church, I am not speaking of churches individually, rather I use the term *Church of Alief* as a whole body of churches.

Important Note: Furthermore, the phrase *Church of Alief* does not refer to any one church, denomination, or association of churches; rather, it refers to the spiritual aspect in which all the Christ-believing churches in the area represent the presence of God.

Ezekiel 8:14–15

> *Then he brought me to the entrance of the north gate of the LORD's house, and I saw women sitting there weeping for Tammuz. And he said to me, "Do you see this, son of man? You will see even more detestable acts than these."*

We now get to the third location, something that is worse than the first two places where God took Ezekiel. In this passage, we find ourselves at the door of the gate of the Lord's house. God shows Ezekiel women who are weeping for an idol named Tammuz. You get a sense of God's displeasure when He simply asks Ezekiel, "Do you see this?" What is so bad about what they were doing in their worship for Tammuz that it makes it even worse than religious leaders going astray?

Tammuz worship originated in Phoenicia and spread to Greece, where the name of Tammuz was changed to Adonis. According to the *New Encyclopedia Britannica,* Tammuz was a "god of fertility embodying the powers for new life in nature in the spring."[1] Tammuz worship centered around two annual festivals; one celebrated his return to life and the other mourned his death. The activities at each of these yearly festivals centered around Baal-like worship and temple prostitution. What Ezekiel saw were women who were "mourning" the death of their god by prostituting themselves and participating in very vile sexual acts. As I was researching this, I must admit I was amazed at how mourning Tammuz's death and celebrating his return to life mimics the observances of the death, burial, and resurrection of our Savior, the Lord Jesus Christ. Satan has always had a counterfeit religion that appeals to the flesh.

Correlation to Alief

No one can pinpoint exactly when it happened, but sometime between 1996 and 2009, the street of Bissonnet in Alief became synonymous with prostitution and sex trafficking. We have had the opportunity to interview several young women about why they are prostituting themselves. By far, most of them say they do it for the

money they earn. It seems that just as Tammuz's name was changed to Adonis when he was adopted by Greece, his name was changed to "Money" here. While we believe that all people who are prostituting themselves are essentially victims, very few verbalized that to us, and fewer still admitted to resorting to such acts just to survive. Most of them seemed proud of their prostitution because of the amounts of money earned and prouder still for being able to list all the pastors and deacons they had as customers. Let me give this warning: if the day ever comes when all the photos I've seen on some of these prostitutes' cell phones were made public, a lot of Houston's religious leaders would be in trouble, and the local body of Christ would suffer in reputation. According to what God is showing Ezekiel, this type of sexual activity in a region and among God's people is just another proof that His blessing is lifting or has already lifted.

Ezekiel 8:16–18

> *So he brought me to the inner court of the LORD's house, and there were about twenty-five men at the entrance of the LORD's temple, between the portico and the altar, with their*

> *backs to the LORD's temple and their faces turned to the east. They were bowing to the east in worship of the sun. And he said to me, "Do you see this, son of man? Is it not enough for the house of Judah to commit the detestable acts they are doing here, that they must also fill the land with violence and repeatedly anger me, even putting the branch to their nose? Therefore I will respond with wrath. I will not show pity or spare them. Though they call loudly in my hearing, I will not listen to them."*

Next, we find ourselves in a most holy spot, between the porch and the altar of the temple. What we find there is something God tells Ezekiel is even worse than Tummuz worship. Ezekiel was brought into the inner court of the Lord's house where the priests were before the altar. Ezekiel sees that the priests have turned their back on God and are worshipping something else entirely, in this case, the sun. Because the priests have turned their back on God, the land is filled with violence (the word can also be translated to "injustice"), and because of their practice of putting the "branch to their nose," they have provoked God to anger. There is not a consensus among commentators as to what "putting the branch to the nose" means. However, in every commentary, it is not a good thing. If I were to summarize most of the commentaries, I'd say that "putting the branch to the nose" was a form of submission to the thing you were worshipping.

Correlation to Alief

This is the very definition of the warning Paul gave Timothy concerning pastors that would invade the flock in the following passages from 2 Timothy:

> *But know this: Hard times will come in the last days. For people will be lovers of self, lovers of money, boastful, proud, demeaning, disobedient to parents, ungrateful, unholy, unloving, irreconcilable, slanderers, without self-control, brutal, without love for what is good, traitors, reckless, conceited, lovers of pleasure rather than lovers of God, holding to the form of godliness but denying its power. Avoid these people.*
>
> *For among them are those who worm their way into households and deceive gullible women overwhelmed by sins and led astray by a variety of passions, always learning and never able to come to a knowledge of the truth. Just as Jannes*

and Jambres resisted Moses, so these also resist the truth. They are men who are corrupt in mind and worthless in regard to the faith. But they will not make further progress, for their foolishness will be clear to all, as was the foolishness of Jannes and Jambres. But you have followed my teaching, conduct, purpose, faith, patience, love, and endurance, along with the persecutions and sufferings that came to me in Antioch, Iconium, and Lystra. What persecutions I endured—and yet the Lord rescued me from them all. In fact, all who want to live a godly life in Christ Jesus will be persecuted. Evil people and impostors will become worse, deceiving and being deceived.

—2 Tim. 3:1–13

I solemnly charge you before God and Christ Jesus, who is going to judge the living and the dead, and because of his appearing and his kingdom: Preach the word; be ready in season and out of season; correct, rebuke, and encourage with great patience and teaching. For the time will come when people will not tolerate sound doctrine, but according to their own desires, will multiply teachers for themselves because they have an itch to hear what they want to hear.

> *They will turn away from hearing the truth and will turn aside to myths.*
>
> —2 Tim. 4:1–4

We are given a similar warning in Jude 1:4–19. Again, it is very important to note that I am not speaking of all pastors or churches in Alief; rather, I am speaking about the condition of the "Church of Alief." Nevertheless, the men mentioned by Paul and Jude are alive and well in the Alief community and are donning the pulpits of churches of all sizes—mega, large, medium, and small. The stories we received from the community, newspaper articles, and copies of texts and pictures prove this beyond a shadow of a doubt.

The body of Christ in Alief is in danger of encountering the provoked anger of God (Ezekiel 8:17). We will see how God carries out his anger in a brief summary of Ezekiel 9 later. As you read this, please pray for pastors everywhere (not just in Alief) that they would turn back to God and that the false pastors would be exposed.

Reflections

PART 3
WITHDRAWAL OF GOD'S INFLUENCE AND THE INFLUX OF INJUSTICE AND OPPRESSION

In this section we will cover:

- understanding the dispersion of the coals in Ezekiel 10:2,
- God's presence going from the temple to the city (region), allowing the influx of injustice and oppression, and
- the meaning of God's presence going to rest on the mountain.

Ezekiel 9

What we have seen thus far is the removal of God's presence from the temple because of the people's actions inside the temple. As God's presence is lifting, He carries out judgment on the region beginning at the temple. This "removing of the candle stick" through the judgment process is detailed in Ezekiel 9.

To accomplish His purpose of carrying out judgment, God calls on "those that have charge over the city." Six men present themselves to God and are each given tasks to accomplish. According to verse 6, they are instructed to start their tasks at the Sanctuary of God. Upon looking at their tasks and how they performed them, it is clear that these men were in fact not men, but angels. What is important to note here is that these angels have charge over the city. This is the first time we see that angels are given territorial control over entire cities (in verse 1 the word for "charge" in Hebrew can be translated as "oversight, care, or custody"). These angels start their tasks at the temple and then carry them out throughout the entire city. Once their tasks in the temple and the city are complete, they return to God and ultimately depart with Him in chapters 10–11.

Important note to remember: Seeing that God's angels (six total for this city) had custody over this entire city and region is important. After these angels depart with the presence of God, who or what will fill the spiritual power vacuum in the coming chapters of Ezekiel?

Hint: Remember the boardroom dreams!

Understanding the Dispersion of the Coals in Ezekiel 10:2

Ezekiel 10–11

In these two chapters we see the complete departure of the presence of God not only from the temple but also from the city. The book of Ezekiel is replete with theological truths and doctrines that would keep even the most astute theological minds occupied for a long time. Since we are focusing on only a very small portion of Ezekiel, I admonish you to read the entire book; you'll especially love the last chapter!

Before the presence of God departs from the temple, He does something special in verse 2 of chapter 10 that we must deal with. He asks the man (angel) clothed in linen to take coals from under the throne of God that was being carried by the cherubim as described in chapter 10:1–2 and scatter them over the city. (This is the same angel described in Ezekiel 9:3–4 who was asked to show God's grace to those who were not part of the idol worship and abomination going on in the land by marking them.) What makes this special is that the man clothed in linen was able to touch the coals and not get burned or destroyed. The only example we have of the coals of the altar of God being handled comes from Isaiah 6, where another type of angel, a seraphim, had to pick up the coal with tongs and, having touched the lips of Isaiah, purge him from sin. When we compare these two events from Ezekiel 10 and Isaiah 6, we see two differences:

- The angel at the throne of God in Ezekiel was able to pick up the coals from the throne with his bare hands and give them to the "man in linen" who also was able to handle the coals with his bare hands. In Ezekiel 10:7 we learn that the angel who was able to take the coals with his bare hands was a cherub. It should not surprise us that a cherub is able to touch the coals at God's throne because Satan himself was a cherub. In fact, he was God's covering cherub and walked up and down in the coals. Read Ezekiel 28 for the chilling story of Lucifer's fall. Cherubs, being a different class of angels than seraphim, must be able to directly touch and handle these coals.

- When the “man in linen” was handed the coals, we hear no mention of his iniquities being purged as we heard when Isaiah’s lips were touched with just one coal in Isaiah 6. Not only that, but Isaiah did not (and could not) directly hold or handle a coal from the throne of God as we see the “man in linen” doing. No tools were needed in Ezekiel 10; both the cherub and the “man in linen” were able to handle these coals with their bare hands.

What’s the Significance of the Man Clothed in Linen?

I’m glad you asked! All we know about this “man clothed in linen” is found in Ezekiel 9 and 10. In Ezekiel 9, this man was responsible for dispatching God’s mercy and grace on those who had chosen God instead of idols (Ezekiel 9:1–11). We also know from his introduction in Ezekiel 9 that he is wearing linen. This is important because no mention is made as to what the other angels wore, which means that his garment is distinctly different from that of the other angels and is worth our attention. Reading Exodus 28 and 39, we learn that linen garments were what the priests wore while performing priestly duties. Also, Ezekiel 44:15–17 explains the importance of linen garments for priestly duties.

Let's pose a question: Is it possible that whoever this "man clothed in linen" was, he is performing a priestly duty before God? We can only answer this question by looking at the duty the "man clothed in linen" was tasked with. As God's wrath was about to be delivered, the "man clothed in linen" was asked to hurry and save all those who chose God over the abominations of the land by marking them to identify them as followers of God. According to the instructions for completing this task in Ezekiel 9, he was supposed to go through the entire population beginning at the sanctuary of God and mark all those he found that fit the description of "men (people) that sigh and cry because of all the abominations." In other words, he had to intercede for all those who believed and set them apart by marking them so that when God's wrath came, they would be passed over. Does that sound familiar?

Theologically speaking, it's clear that this is a "theophany" or an experience with the "pre-incarnate" Christ. For the person who is unfamiliar with either of these two terms, I suggest you do a search on these terms using your favorite internet search engine and enjoy an exciting study into all the times when Christ appeared in the Old Testament. This is an exciting fact to understand since we can see the "pre-incarnate" Christ perform part of His function as a priest, before the book of Hebrews informs us about the priestly duties Jesus performs for us now. Just exciting!

Why Are the Coals Important, and Are They Significant to Our Communities?

To understand the purpose of the coals in Ezekiel 10:2, we need to decide what these coals mean: Were they a form of judgment, or was this a show of grace and mercy from God? Looking at the evidence laid out above, I submit to you that this disbursement of coals in the city was a show of grace and mercy from God. Consider these facts; then we will correlate them to Alief before we move on:

- God always leaves a remnant. We know from the story of Ezra (see Ezra 9) that God had left a remnant of people who follow Him and allowed them a space of grace for the purpose of revival. Realizing this, Ezra led the people to a complete turnaround and revival back to God. Also, in Ezekiel 14:21, God tells Ezekiel that after the "four sore" judgments come (i.e., the sword, the famine, the noisome beast, and the pestilence), a remnant shall be brought forth. Furthermore, when Ezekiel sees their "ways and doings," he will be comforted from his sadness seeing the destruction that God has brought on the land and the people because of their abominations.

- God's physical presence was gone, but He was still there. The coals that were dispersed throughout the city represented God's holiness whether they are under the throne of God or not. These coals scattered throughout the city represented God's diminished manifested presence but also gave the remnant (saved by the "man in linen") a way to connect with God and keep their ways and doings. When the temple was no longer a place where God dwelled, He scattered His holiness among the remnant of the people. We don't know how many coals were scattered, nor do we know how many people made up the remnant. What is important to see here is that while God's physical presence no longer dwelled in a building (the temple), He left scattered around the entire city "holy coals" from His throne, which represented His presence though not actually being Him. The remnant most likely worshipped God in small pockets of the city in the same place where these coals were left.

Correlation to Alief

Remember, I first came to Alief in the 1980s, 1986 to be exact. The presence of God was thick in the Alief community; churches were full, and people were getting saved every single Sunday. No area of the city was known for prostitution; drugs were not a problem, and racism was not as prevalent. As I said earlier, the years between 1996 and 2009 saw an extreme diminishing of God's presence because of the offenses caused by the church leaders as described earlier. The many healthy, thriving churches that once filled Alief have turned into a handful of mega-churches, most of which are inwardly focused, and just a few small Bible-centered congregations are struggling to survive. Today, if you drove around Alief, you'd see churches everywhere. Some shopping centers have several churches as occupants; at last count, the city has eight megachurches (3,500 members or higher) and countless locations where churches have decided to either close or move outside Alief. With so many churches still operating within the 14.13-square-mile area that is Alief, it begs the question, "Why so much darkness?"

This is why it is important to understand the coals! Not every church, mega or otherwise, carries a coal left behind when God's obvious and manifested presence began to diminish in Alief, between the years of 1996 and 2009. This helps explain "why so much darkness" despite the existence of so many churches in Alief (and other communities on the verge of God's departure in the greater Houston area).

We will explain this in more detail when we address the question posed earlier: "Who will fill the spiritual power vacuum left when God's presence departs a region?"

Reflections

PART 4
GOD'S PRESENCE GOES FROM THE TEMPLE TO THE CITY TO THE MOUNTAIN

In the early days of coal mining before safety standards were as they are today, miners would use canaries to gauge the safety of the atmosphere in the mine. The miners could not detect dangerous gases, such as carbon monoxide or methane, that could accumulate in the mine. Instead, they enlisted the "miner's canary" for its extreme sensitivity to dangerous gases. These small birds alerted the miners to the danger of a poisonous atmosphere by acting erratically or by dying. This would give the miners time to evacuate the mine, fix the problem, and then return to continue working in the mine.

This safety precaution is a great example as we begin to look at the sensitivity of the presence of God in the midst of a sin-filled atmosphere or society:

> *He said to me, "Son of man, do you see what they are doing here—more detestable acts that the house of Israel is committing—so that I must depart from my sanctuary? You will see even more detestable acts."*

Ezekiel 8:6

Here God tells Ezekiel that He has to leave His sanctuary because of the overabundance of sin in the temple. We ought to care about what happens in our churches and in the lives of pastors, since pastors should be examples of a life of faith and godliness to all those learning from us (1 Timothy 4:12).

Ask yourself: *Are there signs of God's diminishing presence in your local churches?* There is no one singular verse we can turn to for a clear progression of God's presence departing a local church or a group of churches like in Alief. However, we can look at the activities in Ezekiel and see that sin had become commonplace, especially among the leadership.

Paul gave Timothy this advice concerning the importance of making sure the leadership in the church of God remained godly and pure. I'm focusing on the leadership when it comes to the presence of God in any local church because Paul seemed very concerned about it. Look at these two passages as he admonishes Timothy, concerning how his leadership directly affects the body of Christ:

1 Timothy 3:14–15

> *I write these things to you, hoping to come to you soon. But if I should be delayed, I have written so that you will know how people ought to conduct themselves in God's household, which is the church of the living God, the pillar and foundation of the truth.*

1 Timothy 4:12–16

> *Don't let anyone despise your youth, but set an example for the believers in speech, in conduct, in love, in faith, and in purity. Until I come, give your attention to public reading, exhortation, and teaching. Don't neglect the gift that is in you; it was given to you through*

> *prophecy, with the laying on of hands by the council of elders. Practice these things; be committed to them, so that your progress may be evident to all. Pay close attention to your life and your teaching; persevere in these things, for in doing this you will save both yourself and your hearers.*

Consider the comment of my good friend and brother Pastor Kevin Riser: "Doctrine and the practicing of that doctrine matter. For the light of God to truly shine in a believer, both doctrine and living out that doctrine matter (faith and works)."

2 Timothy 4:1–4

> *I solemnly charge you before God and Christ Jesus, who is going to judge the living and the dead, and because of his appearing and his kingdom: Preach the word; be ready in season and out of season; correct, rebuke, and encourage with great patience and teaching. For the time will come when people will not tolerate sound doctrine, but according to their own desires, will multiply teachers for*

> *themselves because they have an itch to hear what they want to hear. They will turn away from hearing the truth and will turn aside to myths.*

In conclusion of this point, the quality of Timothy's spiritual life as a leader had a direct impact on all those who were under his pastorship (1 Timothy 4:16). Also, Timothy was to make sure he always taught the Word in a way that would reprove, rebuke, and exhort—i.e., provide accountability. If there is no spiritual accountability coming from the sermons out of the pulpit and if the pastor's spiritual life is out of alignment with the Word of God for how a pastor should live, I can safely conclude that the presence of God is diminishing or has diminished in that church.

An Important Note: Neither the size of a church's membership nor the excitement about the sounds of its worship team is an accurate measure of God's presence.

Once God's Presence Departs the Temple, He Goes into the City

We know from Ezekiel 11:23 that as God's presence heads toward the mountains, it lifts from "the midst of the city." But before He left, He took Ezekiel on a tour of the city in Ezekiel 11.

Why Is Looking Upon the City Important?

That's a good question and worthy of some commentary. The first thing we notice is who is prominent in the mischief in the city: leaders. Ezekiel says there were "twenty-five men. Among them I saw Jaazaniah the son of Azzur, and Pelatiah son of Benaiah, leaders of the people" (Ezek. 11:1).

These men were leaders in the city, ranking all the way to a prince. Without the standards and convictions that should have been taught and demonstrated by God's priests, these men were left to their own devices and mischief. I'm not making a case for merging "church and state"; rather I'm pointing out that when godless people take office and lead a city, they tend to do less godly things.

Also, because of the immoral actions coming out of the temple, these men were able to conduct their wickedness from the very grounds of the temple, and in fact, in partnership with the priests in it (Ezekiel 11:1). Truly, the condition of the land, any land, is directly related to the condition of God's people.

2 Chronicles 7:12–14

> *Then the* Lord *appeared to Solomon at night and said to him: "I have heard your*

> *prayer and have chosen this place for myself as a temple of sacrifice. If I shut the sky so there is no rain, or if I command the grasshopper to consume the land, or if I send pestilence on my people, and my people, who bear my name, humble themselves, pray and seek my face, and turn from their evil ways, then I will hear from heaven, forgive their sin, and heal their land."*

The influx of injustice and oppression can only happen in an environment where God's manifested glory (presence) is no longer dwelling in the temple, nor among His people because of their involvement in sin. This in turn opens the door for all kinds of sin to run rampant and unchecked, thereby oppressing the entire region. Paul warns Timothy that times like this could occur at any moment, and thus his warning sign would be the quality of the spiritual life of those in leadership—whether they were walking in holiness or not. In contrast, Timothy was to be an example of purity to all those around him. In doing so, he would save himself and those who followed him (1 Tim. 4:16).

Other Warnings of the Importance of the Spiritual Health of Leadership

Second Peter, Jeremiah, and Titus contain other warnings about the importance of having spiritual health in leadership:

2 Peter 2:1–3

> *There were indeed false prophets among the people, just as there will be false teachers among you. They will bring in destructive heresies, even denying the Master who bought them, and will bring swift destruction on themselves. Many will follow their depraved ways, and the way of truth will be maligned because of them. They will exploit you in their greed with made-up stories. Their condemnation, pronounced long ago, is not idle, and their destruction does not sleep.*

Jeremiah 23:1–2

> *"Woe to the shepherds who destroy and scatter the sheep of my pasture!" This is the* Lord*'s declaration. "Therefore, this is what*

the Lord, *the God of Israel, says about the shepherds who tend my people: You have scattered my flock, banished them, and have not attended to them. I am about to attend to you because of your evil acts"—this is the* Lord*'s declaration.*

Titus 1:7–11

As an overseer of God's household, he must be blameless: not arrogant, not hot-tempered, not an excessive drinker, not a bully, not greedy for money, but hospitable, loving what is good, sensible, righteous, holy, self-controlled, holding to the faithful message as taught, so that he will be able both to encourage with sound teaching and to refute those who contradict it. For there are many rebellious people, full of empty talk and deception, especially those from the circumcision party. It is necessary to silence them; they are ruining entire households by teaching what they shouldn't in order to get money dishonestly.

The Meaning of God's Presence Going to Rest on the Mountain

According to Ezekiel 11:23, the presence of God remained or endured on the mountain: *"The glory of the LORD rose up from within the city and stopped on the mountain east of the city."* The word *stopped* is used in the Christian Standard Bible; the word *stood* is used in the ESV, NASB, and KJV. In the Hebrew, the word is *amad* [aw-mad], which means "to remain, endure or to take one's stand."

God has removed His glory from the people, the temple, and the city, and is now occupying the mountains on the city's east side. We never hear of God drawing away any further. He remains upon the mountain until He redeems His people in the later chapters of Ezekiel.

Now, we need to understand why God moved His glory (presence) to the mountain and kept it there. It's in this understanding that we will comprehend the strategy needed to regain what we've lost.

Ever since the flood of Noah's day, the mountains have represented a place where God resides and is served and worshipped. It was this historical understanding that Jesus corrected when He met the Samaritan woman in John 4:15–24. She thought God still resided in the mountains and was not aware that God, being a Spirit, must be worshipped in spirit and in truth, not in a set location. Jesus taught her that the glory of God was going to dwell with man once again, and indeed was already present in Jesus Christ, the Messiah.

While we will not make the same mistake she made in relegating God to one location, we will show a very important precedent set in scripture, regarding God and the mountains. Here I offer brief explanations of just a few passages of scripture that highlight this precedent. We'll end with a more in-depth explanation of how this precedent is revealed in Ezekiel and how we can use it to set our strategy for bringing freedom to Alief.

Genesis 8:1–5, 20

After the flood, Noah built an alter on the mountain to worship God; this is the first time an altar was built to worship God on a mountain.

> *God remembered Noah, as well as all the wildlife and all the livestock that were with him in the ark. God caused a wind to pass over the earth, and the water began to subside. The sources of the watery depths and the floodgates of the sky were closed, and the*

> *rain from the sky stopped. The water steadily receded from the earth, and by the end of 150 days the water had decreased significantly. The ark came to rest in the seventh month, on the seventeenth day of the month, on the mountains of Ararat. The water continued to recede until the tenth month; in the tenth month, on the first day of the month, the tops of the mountains were visible. Then Noah built an altar to the LORD. He took some of every kind of clean animal and every kind of clean bird and offered burnt offerings on the altar.*

Exodus 3:1–12

God revealed Himself to Moses for the first time, on the "mountain of God." God instructed Moses for the next season of his life and told him that the people, once they were brought out of Egypt, would come to the same mountain where God was abiding at the time and worship Him there:

> *Meanwhile, Moses was shepherding the flock of his father-in-law Jethro, the priest of Midian. He led the flock to the far side of the wil-*

derness and came to Horeb, the mountain of God. Then the angel of the L*ORD appeared to him in a flame of fire within a bush. As Moses looked, he saw that the bush was on fire but was not consumed. So Moses thought, "I must go over and look at this remarkable sight. Why isn't the bush burning up?" When the* LORD *saw that he had gone over to look, God called out to him from the bush, "Moses, Moses!" "Here I am," he answered. "Do not come closer," he said. "Remove the sandals from your feet, for the place where you are standing is holy ground." Then he continued, "I am the God of your father, the God of Abraham, the God of Isaac, and the God of Jacob." Moses hid his face because he was afraid to look at God. Then the* LORD *said, "I have observed the misery of my people in Egypt, and have heard them crying out because of their oppressors. I know about their sufferings, and I have come down to rescue them from the power of the Egyptians and to bring them from that land to a good and spacious land, a land flowing with milk and honey—the ter-*

ritory of the Canaanites, Hethites, Amorites, Perizzites, Hivites, and Jebusites. So because the Israelites' cry for help has come to me, and I have also seen the way the Egyptians are oppressing them, therefore, go. I am sending you to Pharaoh so that you may lead my people, the Israelites, out of Egypt."

But Moses asked God, "Who am I that I should go to Pharaoh and that I should bring the Israelites out of Egypt?" He answered, "I will certainly be with you, and this will be the sign to you that I am the one who sent you: when you bring the people out of Egypt, you will all worship God at this mountain."

Exodus 24:12–18

After the Israelites were delivered from Egypt, they came to the mountain. God personally invited Moses to go up on the mount to be with Him, so that Moses could receive instruction for the people:

The Lord said to Moses, "Come up to me on the mountain and stay there so that I may give you the stone tablets with the law

> *and commandments I have written for their instruction." So Moses arose with his assistant Joshua and went up the mountain of God. He told the elders, "Wait here for us until we return to you. Aaron and Hur are here with you. Whoever has a dispute should go to them." When Moses went up the mountain, the cloud covered it. The glory of the LORD settled on Mount Sinai, and the cloud covered it for six days. On the seventh day he called to Moses from the cloud. The appearance of the LORD's glory to the Israelites was like a consuming fire on the mountaintop. Moses entered the cloud as he went up the mountain, and he remained on the mountain forty days and forty nights.*

Isaiah 2:1–3

Isaiah prophesied concerning the last days. In those days, people and all nations will go to the mountain of the Lord to get instruction, learn the ways of God, and learn how to walk in His paths:

> *The vision that Isaiah son of Amoz saw concerning Judah and Jerusalem: In the last*

> *days the mountain of the LORD's house will be established at the top of the mountains and will be raised above the hills. All nations will stream to it, and many peoples will come and say, "Come, let us go up to the mountain of the LORD, to the house of the God of Jacob. He will teach us about his ways so that we may walk in his paths." For instruction will go out of Zion and the word of the LORD from Jerusalem.*

Isaiah 56:1–7

Here, God extends His covenant to all who obey, not just the Jews. One of the benefits found in verse 7 is that God will bring us into His presence **in the mountain**, where we will be made joyful in God's house of prayer. At the end of verse 7, God says, "for mine house shall be called an house of prayer for all people" (KJV). It's interesting to note, that this house of prayer is located in the mountain!

> *This is what the LORD says: Preserve justice and do what is right, for my salvation is coming soon, and my righteousness will be revealed. Happy is the person who does this,*

the son of man who holds it fast, who keeps the Sabbath without desecrating it, and keeps his hand from doing any evil.

No foreigner who has joined himself to the LORD *should say, "The* LORD *will exclude me from his people," and the eunuch should not say, "Look, I am a dried-up tree." For the* LORD *says this: "For the eunuchs who keep my Sabbaths, and choose what pleases me, and hold firmly to my covenant, I will give them, in my house and within my walls, a memorial and a name better than sons and daughters. I will give each of them an everlasting name that will never be cut off. As for the foreigners who join themselves to the* LORD *to minister to him, to love the name of the* LORD*, and to become his servants—all who keep the Sabbath without desecrating it and who hold firmly to my covenant—I will bring them to my holy mountain and let them rejoice in my house of prayer. Their burnt offerings and sacrifices will be acceptable on my altar, for my house will be called a house of prayer for all nations."*

The following passage tells us clearly, that in the last days, the house of the Lord will be in the mountains and that **all** nations will come to the house of the Lord in the mountains to learn and receive instruction in the ways of the Lord:

> *In the last days the mountain of the LORD's house will be established at the top of the mountains and will be raised above the hills. Peoples will stream to it, and many nations will come and say, "Come, let's go up to the mountain of the LORD, to the house of the God of Jacob. He will teach us about his ways so we may walk in his paths." For instruction will go out of Zion and the word of the LORD from Jerusalem.*
>
> —Micah 4:1–2

Matthew 14:23

Here, we see Jesus alone on the mountain praying. Often when Jesus was asked why He was doing something, His answer would be that He was only doing as His Father instructed Him to do; He received those instructions on the mountain:

> *After dismissing the crowds, he went up on the mountain by himself to pray. Well into the night, he was there alone.*

Ezekiel 20:36–44

Finally, let's look at how this precedent is revealed in the portion of Ezekiel, which shows us that no matter how long we have been apart from God and indulged in all kinds of sin, it is still His desire that we come to Him in His mountain. And when we come to God in repentance, He reminds us of who we are by showing us how far we have fallen, causing us to "loathe" ourselves because of all the corrupt acts we have done (verse 43). This must be how David felt about his sin in Psalms 51. Second, the passage reminds us of who God is after He has dealt with us according to His grace for His name's sake (verse 44).

> *Just as I entered into judgment with your ancestors in the wilderness of the land of Egypt, so I will enter into judgment with you. This is the declaration of the LORD GOD. I will make you pass under the rod and will bring you into the bond of the covenant. I will purge you of those who rebel and transgress against me. I will bring them out of the land where they live as foreign residents, but they will not enter the land of Israel. Then you will know that I am the LORD.*

"'As for you, house of Israel, this is what the LORD GOD says: Go and serve your idols, each of you. But afterward you will surely listen to me, and you will no longer defile my holy name with your gifts and idols. For on my holy mountain, Israel's high mountain—the declaration of the LORD GOD—there the entire house of Israel, all of them, will serve me in the land. There I will accept them and will require your contributions and choicest gifts, all your holy offerings. When I bring you from the peoples and gather you from the countries where you have been scattered, I will accept you as a pleasing aroma. And I will demonstrate my holiness through you in the sight of the nations. When I lead you into the land of Israel, the land I swore to give your fathers, you will know that I am the LORD. There you will remember your ways and all your deeds by which you have defiled yourself, and you will loathe yourselves for all the evil things you have done. You will know that I am the LORD, house of Israel, when I have dealt with you for the sake of my name

> *rather than according to your evil ways and corrupt acts. This is the declaration of the* LORD GOD.'"

It would seem that when God cannot dwell in and among His people because of the presence of sin, He withdraws to the mountain where we must go to Him to be cleansed, refreshed, revived, transformed, forgiven, instructed, and be given back all that we have lost.

> *I lift my eyes toward the mountains. Where will my help come from? My help comes from the* LORD*, the Maker of heaven and earth.*
>
> —Ps. 121:1–2

Since it is obvious that God's presence has diminished in our community, a few questions must be answered:

- Could God be waiting for us to join Him "in the mountain"? If so, where is the mountain today?
- Since God is not relegated to a single spot (a literal mountain), where must we go to be with God "in His mountain"? Good question! This will be answered in the section on receiving a strategy from God. However, we can answer the next question now!

- Is it possible that since 1996 (when the Alief community first began to experience the diminished presence of God according to our research), the local body of Christ has forgotten the fullness of who we truly are? Has the fight to keep churches open and functioning taken the place of having a passion for God because we do not know who we are?

Research from the Barna Group published in 2018 gives some very surprising answers to our questions:

- "Rates of church attendance, religious affiliation, belief in God, prayer and Bible-reading have been dropping for decades. Americans' beliefs are becoming more post-Christian and, concurrently, religious identity is changing."[2]
- "Generation Z: Born between 1999 and 2015, is the first truly 'post-Christian' generation. More than any other generation before, the Gen Z does not assert a religious identity."[3]

A 2006 Barna research paper showed the following trends:

- "In total, six out of ten twenty somethings were involved in a church during their teen years, but have failed to translate that into active spirituality during their early adulthood."[4]
- "A majority of twenty somethings—61% of today's young adults—had been churched at one point during their teen years, but they are now spiritually disengaged."[5]

I want to point out an extremely important point here. Is it any wonder that the first ever "post-Christian" generation was born during the same time frame as the spiritual decline in Alief? Could it be that during the same time frame in cities all over the world, Satan was making a huge, coordinated move to cause the body of Christ to fall away? No matter your answer, we must deal with this fact: the children of the people who were part of the "great fall of Alief" are considered "post-Christian," and they are being held hostage to the great bondage of sin that is prevalent in my community.

Reflections

PART 5
WE AREN'T JUST DEALING WITH DEMONIC FORCES IN PEOPLE

In my opening statement of this book, I said: "A satanically depressed area can be described as one where a region or territory is occupied by fallen angels without much contention from forces of light (the body of Christ). The goal is to control an entire region in order to control the people within it."

I then explained the strategy of having territorial control of a region and its importance in warfare. In this section, I will provide biblical examples of an entire region that was controlled by satanic forces and explain why it is important to understand that we are not dealing with people under the control of Satan, but we are dealing with a territory under oppression.

Where in the Bible are there examples of "spirits of evil" oppressing an area, causing people to leave God and enter vile lives of sin?

Hosea 4:12

> *My people consult their wooden idols, and their divining rods inform them. For a spirit of promiscuity leads them astray; they act promiscuously in disobedience to their God.*

Hosea 5:3–4

> *I know Ephraim, and Israel is not hidden from me. For now, Ephraim, you have acted promiscuously; Israel is defiled. Their actions do not allow them to return to their God, for a spirit of promiscuity is among them, and they do not know the LORD.*

These two passages show that not only was the "spirit of promiscuity" in the midst of the land (Hosea 5:4), but it was causing the people to sin and leave God even to the point where they no longer knew God. How could the "spirit of promiscuity" or any spirit for that matter, take over an entire region and cause the people of God to fall away so far, and so fast?

Hosea 4:1–11

> *Hear the word of the LORD, people of Israel, for the LORD has a case against the inhabitants of the land: There is no truth, no faithful love, and no knowledge of God in the land! Cursing, lying, murder, stealing, and adultery are rampant; one act of bloodshed follows another. For this reason the land mourns, and everyone who lives in it languishes, along with the wild animals and the birds of the sky; even the fish of the sea disappear. But let no one dispute; let no one argue, for my case is against you priests. You will stumble by day; the prophet will also stumble with you by night. And I will destroy your mother. My people are destroyed for lack of knowledge. Because you have rejected knowledge, I will reject you from serving as my priest. Since you have forgotten the law of your God, I will also forget your sons.*

> *The more they multiplied, the more they sinned against me. I will change their honor into disgrace. They feed on the sin of my people; they have an appetite for their iniquity. The same judgment will happen to both people and priests. I will punish them for their ways and repay them for their deeds. They will eat but not be satisfied; they will be promiscuous but not multiply. For they have abandoned their devotion to the LORD. Promiscuity, wine, and new wine take away one's understanding.*

In verses 1–10 of this passage, we see that God had a controversy with the inhabitants of the land because of the vile sins they were committing. In fact, because of their actions the whole region was oppressed by their sin even to the point that the animals were suffering. But still, these are just the results, or the consequences if you will, of the people of the land committing sin. In fact, we learn in verses 1 and 6 that the priests carry most of the responsibility for this widespread sin. Why? Because there was no truth in the land and the people had no knowledge of God. This played a big part in the downward spiral of this land.

Still, the bigger question must be answered here: How did this happen? Verse 11 gives us an indication of what happened: promiscuity and alcohol had taken away their heart, and verse 12 tells us that the problem was rooted in spiritual warfare. The "spirit of whoredoms" with the help of alcohol territorially oppressed this entire region to the point that the people began to fall until there was no indication that they were God's people.

It is interesting to note that alcohol and drunkenness in leadership allowed the "spirit of whoredoms" to oppress the region and the people so badly that they did not even know they were oppressed. Is it any wonder that Paul, when giving Timothy the instructions for the qualifications for leadership in the body of Christ, told Timothy that the leaders must not be lovers of strong drink (alcohol)? If you have any question about the culpability of leadership in the situation mentioned in Hosea, read Hosea 5:1, where God lays a direct charge against the priests.

We see this example and pattern again in Jeremiah 23:1–2 and 11–13 where the Old Testament pastors, prophets, and priests left the truth and caused the people to stray.

Is It Possible to Defeat "Spirits of Evil" That Have Oppressed a Region?

To answer that question, we must take note of a few important examples:

- Every example of Jesus defeating a demonic force was a demon in a person, never a territorial demon.
- The same is also true for all the occurrences when the apostles had authority over a demonic force to cast it out. It was always in a person; never did we see them exercise authority over territorial demonic forces.
- However, in Daniel 10, we see a territorial demonic force being confronted and defeated by two angels of God: Gabriel and Michael, the archangel. They came in response to Daniel, who was fasting about a vision God had given him. After the prince of the kingdom of Persia (who is widely accepted as being a spiritual reference to a fallen angel) was overcome by the combined forces of Gabriel and Michael. Then Daniel is told that the prince of Grecia (another unnamed fallen angel) will come forth when Gabriel leaves to continue fighting against the prince of Persia.

It is clear that while we have authority over all demonic activity on earth in people, as mentioned before in the examples of Jesus and the early church Apostles, we do not have authority to fight or do warfare with fallen angelic forces fighting in the spiritual realms. According to the example in Daniel, only angels sent by God can fight fallen angels that have taken a territory to oppress it. Just as the archangel Michael outranks Gabriel in the heavenly hierarchy that exists among the heavenly host, there must also exist a ranking system among fallen demonic forces. Those wicked spiritual forces that would possess, or afflict, a person are surely far lower in rank than the fallen angels that have the greater power to take control of an entire geographic region or territory.

Therefore, it is important that we get to "the mountain" and draw close to the presence of God, where He (and His Angel army) will fight this wickedness on our behalf!

Reflections

PART 6
RECEIVING THE STRATEGY

We can now begin to discuss receiving a strategy from God. First, I want to remind you of the unanswered questions that we have yet to address:

1. The first question comes from the section titled "The Withdrawal of God's Influence and the Influx of Injustice and Oppression." After my comments on Ezekiel 9, the question is this: "Who or what will fill the spiritual power vacuum when these angels depart with the presence of God in the coming chapters of Ezekiel?"
2. The second question comes from the section titled "The Meaning of God's Presence Going to Rest

on the Mountain." After my comments on Ezekiel 20:36–44, you find these questions: "Could God be waiting for us to join Him on the mountain? Where is the mountain today? Where must we go to be with God on the mountain?"

Who Will Fill the Spiritual Vacuum?

Having considered the withdrawal of God's influence and the influx of injustice and oppression earlier, we must attempt to answer the following question: Who or what will fill the spiritual power vacuum when these angels depart with the presence of God as described in Ezekiel?

In Matthew 12:43–45 (also in Luke 11:24–26), we get an idea of the type of environment an unclean spirit looks for.

> *When an unclean spirit comes out of a person, it roams through waterless places looking for rest but doesn't find any. Then it says, "I'll go back to my house that I came from." Returning, it finds the house vacant, swept, and put in order. Then it goes and brings with it seven other spirits more evil*

> *than itself, and they enter and settle down there. As a result, that person's last condition is worse than the first. That's how it will also be with this evil generation.*

Not just any available area will do, certain criteria must be met. Let's look at them. First, we see that the demon mentions that it is roaming through "waterless places looking for rest" and that it is not able to find any. Since we are dealing with a demon who wars in the spiritual plane and not in the fleshly (Ephesians 6:12), we must look at the spiritual meaning of the words used to describe the activities of this demon.

The term *waterless* means there is a lack of water wherever this demon is searching. Spiritually speaking, water (in the New Testament) is defined in John 4:7–15 when Jesus has this exchange with the woman at the well and defines *spiritual water* in verse 14:

> *A woman of Samaria came to draw water. "Give me a drink," Jesus said to her, because his disciples had gone into town to buy food. "How is it that you, a Jew, ask for a drink from me, a Samaritan woman?" she asked him. For Jews do not associate with Samaritans.*

> *Jesus answered, "If you knew the gift of God, and who is saying to you, 'Give me a drink,' you would ask him, and he would give you living water." "Sir," said the woman, "you don't even have a bucket, and the well is deep. So where do you get this 'living water'? You aren't greater than our father Jacob, are you? He gave us the well and drank from it himself, as did his sons and livestock." Jesus said, "Everyone who drinks from this water will get thirsty again. But whoever drinks from the water that I will give him will never get thirsty again. In fact, the water I will give him will become a well of water springing up in him for eternal life." "Sir," the woman said to him, "give me this water so that I won't get thirsty and come here to draw water."*

I can comfortably conclude that any place that is dry to a demon is a place that is lacking this "spiritual water springing up into eternal life." In other words, it is a place that lacks the presence and power of God.

This demon, after roaming about for an undisclosed amount of time and being unable to find a suitable place to rest decides to return to the place it originally left and found that it was "vacant, swept, and put in order." This vacancy allowed the demon to invite seven other demons more evil then itself, leaving the person in a worse condition than when this all started. How was this demon able to not only come back, but also invite seven other demons that were more evil than itself?

Answer: power vacuum.

A quick online search of the term *power vacuum* will reveal that this is a condition that occurs when a person in power loses control of that power (or leaves) without assigning a replacement. The vacant seat of authority becomes a power vacuum. As we saw in the story of this young man, the power vacuum will always be filled. In his case since he did not fill the vacuum with "water," it allowed the demon to come back with friends.

As a side note: Jesus understood this principle, which is why, when He ascended, He sent the Holy Spirit to walk with us, filling the power vacuum that would have been left with His absence. Jesus in effect negated any chance for a power vacuum struggle caused by a waterless situation.

Having gone through this passage and seeing these principles as they relate to a person, let's apply them to a territory and answer this question: Who or what will fill the spiritual power vacuum when these angels depart with the presence of God?

In review of Ezekiel 9, we learned that territorial control of a city was given to six angels of God. The power vacuum began when these angels departed and vacated their seats without naming replacements as they departed and left with the presence of God. We ended our discussion of Ezekiel 9 with a hint: "Remember the boardroom dreams!"

God revealed to me in those dreams that Satan and his fallen angels had assumed territorial control over Alief when God's presence diminished between the years of 1996 and 2009, and they had entrenched themselves deep within the area. Their whole goal was to never lose ground and to keep the area oppressed. As it was for Alief, so it was for the land in Ezekiel's time. The existing unfilled power vacuum attracted all kinds of evil and rebellion to the land.

So, we now know the "who" of our question is Satan and his fallen angels. However, I feel it important to address another important question very briefly: "Where did they come from?"

In our example taken from Matthew 12:43–45, we saw that the demon left its "home" looking for another waterless place. We don't know based on the context whether it left willingly or was kicked out; all we know is that it was searching for another area. The point I want to make is that if this demon had found another dwelling place, whoever (or wherever) he had made his new home would be possessed by a demon that came from somewhere else, not a brand-new demon. This demon would have vacated one location and then occupied another. Neither Satan nor his angels are omnipresent (able to be everywhere at all times), and in that regard, they are limited to the number of places they can be. If there aren't enough dry waterless places, they are relegated to what is available. Being omnipresent, God isn't bound in this way; He can and is everywhere, all the time. This would explain why so many demons had to pack into this young man at the end of the story. There just weren't enough available places where they had authority to be. (The story about the pigs in Mark 5:1–13 is another great example showing this principle.) Woe to the person (or community) who becomes home to multiple demons.

Territorially, this begs the following questions:

1. Where did the territorial demons that are now in Alief come from?
2. Where will they go once God finally delivers the Alief area from this oppression?

This is not the book to answer those questions, but it would not surprise me at all if at the same time Alief was becoming satanically oppressed, there was a community somewhere being delivered at the mountain of God and filled with the water of His presence. Also in a proactive sense, is there a way to warn neighboring communities that as God begins to deliver Alief, their community could be probed for its spiritual water content and, if found lacking, they could be next? I challenge someone who hears God's call to research these thoughts and help answer these questions.

At last, we can answer the second question and in so doing discuss and discover a strategy from God on delivering Alief or any satanically depressed area.

Where Do We Go from Here?

Now we're ready to take on our remaining questions from the section titled "The Meaning of God's Presence Going to Rest on the Mountain." Could God be waiting for us to join Him on the mountain? Where is the mountain today? Where must we go to be with God on His mountain? In this final section, our sole goal is to determine what God's strategy is to deliver our area from satanic oppression. We will answer the questions above as we proceed on our discovery journey toward the strategy.

Review of the Mountain

It's imperative that we remember the importance of the mountain in scripture and how we saw it in Ezekiel. This review is so that we can carry over what we learned from that section to this one as we dive deeper.

1. According to Ezekiel 11:23, the manifested presence of God remained and endured on the mountain after leaving the temple and the city.
2. In reviewing the verses from the section on the mountain, we learn an important precedent and pattern:

    Genesis 8:1–5, 20—We saw that God is praised. (This is also the first mention of an altar to God.)

    Exodus 3:1–5 and Exodus 24:1–12—Moses was invited to join God on the mountain to receive instruction for himself in Exodus chapter 3 and for the people in Exodus chapter 24.

    Isaiah 2:1–3—In this prophecy all nations go to the mountain of God to receive instruction in the ways of God and learn to walk in His paths.

Isaiah 56:1–7—God extends His covenant to all who obey Him. God then brings the people to His mountain, into His house of prayer where they will be joyful as they worship, praise, and pray.

Micah 4:1–2—Again, we see a prophecy concerning a future time when people will flock to the "House of the Lord established on the top of the mountains" where they will receive teachings in the ways and paths of God.

Matthew 14:23—Jesus spent most of His personal prayer times on the mountains with God. His daily instructions came from these moments.

Ezekiel 20:36–44—Shows the grace of God toward us and His desire for us to join Him on the mountain. This experience with God must be first initiated with repentance; God then begins to show us and remind us how far we have fallen from His will. Ultimately, God reveals that His grace for us was because of His namesake and that His love for us was not diminished due to our sin.

When we combine all these points into one foundational statement on the purpose of God's mountain, we will have a clear, concise understanding for the rest of this section:

> The mountain of God reflects His manifold wisdom and love for mankind in that while we are sinners and far from Him, God openly invites us to His house of prayer that is established on the top of the mountains. Those who come with hearts of humility and repentance are brought into the fullness of God's joy as they pray, worship, and receive instructions to walk in the paths and ways of God for themselves, their families, and their community.

How Do We Find the Mountain?

To answer this question, we need to investigate how the others from the verses in the previous section found their way there.

Taking the verses in the order that we covered them, we find that Noah found his way there through a heart of praise and worship after coming off the Ark. Moses, having left Egypt and become a shepherd of Jethro's flock, found his way to the mountain of God after being drawn in by the curious notion of a burning bush. God seeing that Moses was drawn in, called him by name, and the rest is history. Having delivered God's people, Moses was invited by God directly to receive instruction for the people.

In Isaiah 2 we see that the people in the prophesied time will have a hunger to learn the ways of God and will flow to the mountain of the Lord knowing that it is the only place to quench their thirst. In Isaiah 56 all people who obey God are brought by God to His holy mountain and into His house of prayer where they will rejoice and worship. Micah 4 speaks of a time to come when many nations will flow to the house of the Lord on the mountain once God establishes it and exalts it above everything else. People will be filled with the desire to learn of the ways, paths, and laws of God. In Matthew 14 we see that whenever Jesus desired to talk to the Father, He had open access to the mountain and an audience in the House of Prayer. Last, in Ezekiel 20 we see that after allowing His people to be disciplined and purging all the rebels and those who were open transgressors, God begins to deal with His people through His holiness and for His namesake, causing the people much conviction and transformation. They came to understand God's great grace in that He did not deal with them according to their sin.

So how does this help us find the mountain? The answer is "categories." As we examine just these few verses dealing with the mountain of God, we see that a pattern of "categories" is established. (I admonish you to look up even more mountain verse to see the same pattern!)

When dealing with individual people, as we saw in the example of Noah, Moses, and Jesus, they encountered God on the mountain through prayer, praise, and a thirst to learn more. When dealing with groups of people, that is, communities or nations, we see that God dealt with them in two different ways:

1. For communities that were obeying and following Him, God brings them to experience the joy of being in the House of Prayer established on the mountain (Isa. 56:1–7).
2. For communities that have fallen into rebellion and sin, God allows destruction and discipline to enter the community or nation and begins to expose those who live in rebellion and sin, driving them out. God then begins to deal with the people's

> sins according to His namesake, not according to their sin. The people in turn go into great repentance and begin to acknowledge God as their Lord again.

Finding the Mountain Depends on Your Category

How you go about finding the mountain depends on your category: find your category, find your strategy.

As a Person

As God promised Elijah, He had reserved a remnant that had not bowed the knee to Baal. I also believe that in every community that is far from God, there exists a remnant that has not bowed the knee. All of them—Noah, Moses, Jesus, and many others—had mountain experiences with God because they desired a relationship with Him. Whether it was praise, worship, repentance, a desire to learn more, or just wanting to talk (prayer), they all found the mountain.

Because you are reading this book, I believe that you have the necessary thirst for God to experience Him on the mountain. Finding the mountain as individuals is your strategy for experiencing personal revival and preparedness for God to call you to join Him in a work that is bigger than you are. Note that no one who visited

God on the mountain remained comfortable in their faith. They were always stretched and pulled to the unfathomable heights of the greatness of God's work.

As a Community/Nation

First you have to decide which of the two descriptions fit your community. If it is the first, your community should be ripe with unity among other local bodies of Christ. The positive influence of the unified local body of Christ will lend itself to improved social order and general well-being of the community. Your strategy should be to remain in constant intercession over the leadership of the unified body of Christ in your community. Being in this category does not make your community safe from future failure. Whether you are a pastor, intercessor, a church leader, or a person interested in spiritual warfare, another part of your strategy is connecting with others who realize that God's presence is resting in and among the community via the combined body of Christ in that area, but who also realize the sensitive nature of the manifest presence of God as we saw in Ezekiel 8:6. The goal is not to just meet and talk, but to become watchmen for the community, praying for church leadership and being sensitive to the spiritual warfare being fought in and over the community together. In unity, you are to become the "miners' canary" that can detect and warn the local body to the dangers that are being manifested spiritually and empirically.

If your community fits the second description, your first goal should be for God to bring the awareness to the Christ community that the plagues ravaging the community are indicative of God's fleeting presence due to the condition of God's people because of the presence of sin. Once God begins revealing the reason behind the plagues, it's time to attract God's presence back to the community and bring deliverance to the area. The book of Joel gives us the perfect outline. In Joel 1, after God speaks to the elders and the inhabitants of the land about the pestilence and plagues, He gives them several steps to follow in verses 8–14, backed up by an awesome promise in chapter 2. Let's look at these steps:

1. Joel 1:8 – *"Grieve like a young woman dressed in sackcloth, mourning for the husband of her youth."* We don't know why but this women's husband is gone, causing her much grief. We, the bride of Christ and, more to the point, the local Bride of Christ of the Alief community are here called to grieve "like" this. We must come to a point of

grief concerning the absence of our husband Jesus Christ in our church and community as a young wife would grieve her husband.

2. Joel 1:11–12 – *"Be ashamed, you farmers, wail, you vinedressers, over the wheat and the barley, because the harvest of the field has perished. The grapevine is dried up, and the fig tree is withered; the pomegranate, the date palm, and the apple—all the trees of the orchard—have withered. Indeed, human joy has dried up."*

   These farmers and vinedressers were told to be ashamed and wail over the condition of the land. Everything they were responsible for—tilling, planting, pruning, and cultivation—had been destroyed or dried up. Jesus left us with fields ripe unto harvest (John 4:35) and promised us that if we (His bride) continued to keep Him lifted up, He would continue to draw more souls. Have we been good farmers, vinedressers, and stewards over our community as Jesus asked us to? Have we, the laborers of the harvest kept Jesus lifted up, or has the focus shifted to one of entertainment and membership retention? Are we, the united local body of Christ in your community ashamed about the reputation of the church in the community? Are you only concerned with your church and not the "church of the community?"

3. Joel 1:9, 13 – *"Grain and drink offerings have been cut off from the house of the LORD; the priests, who are ministers of the LORD, mourn. Dress in sackcloth and lament, you priests; wail, you ministers of the altar. Come and spend the night in sackcloth, you ministers of my God, because grain and drink offerings are withheld from the house of your God."*

   According to verses 9 and 13, the ministers and the priests who are the ones responsible for shepherding the people of God into the presence of God are told to go into deep mourning and lamentation, even to the point of spending the night in sackcloth. The need for such lamenting stems from the fact that the "grain and drink offerings are withheld from the house of God." It's important to understand why the withholding of the offering would cause so much sadness.

   According to Hebrews 10:1, all the ordinances of the law, including the sacrifices, were a "shadow of good things to come." Indeed, these Old Testament sacrifices spoke of Christ and His completion of the law once and for all in Hebrews 10:2–10. Specifically, regarding the "grain and drink" offerings, Jesus spoke of His completion of these in Luke 22:19–20:

> *And he took bread, gave thanks, broke it, gave it to them, and said, "This is my body, which is given for you. Do this in remembrance of me." In the same way he also took the cup after supper and said, "This cup is the new covenant in my blood, which is poured out for you."*

Since this section is not an exhaustive work on the connection between the Old and New Testaments regarding the law and sacrifices, I admonish you to do a deep dive study into the meanings of each sacrifice and how it relates to the church age. The beauty and sadness regarding the "grain and drink" offerings mentioned in Jesus's words from the verses above are found in understanding Numbers 15:1–5:

> *The* LORD *instructed Moses: "Speak to the Israelites and tell them: When you enter the land I am giving you to settle in, and*

> *you make a fire offering to the* LORD *from the herd or flock—either a burnt offering or a sacrifice, to fulfill a vow, or as a freewill offering, or at your appointed festivals—to produce a pleasing aroma for the* LORD*, the one presenting his offering to the* LORD *is also to present a grain offering of two quarts of fine flour mixed with a quart of oil. Prepare a quart of wine as a drink offering with the burnt offering or sacrifice of each lamb."*

We learn here that the "grain and drink" offering must accompany **every** sacrifice offered to God with fire. In the setting of the Lord's Supper, Jesus correlated the beautiful imagery of the willful offering of grain and drink and necessary sacrifices of an animal from the herd or flock with bread and wine with His body and shed blood while saying that we should practice the Lord's Supper in remembrance of His sacrifice. In the Old Testament, if the order and guidelines of the sacrifices were not followed, God would not accept the sacrifice. The priests and ministers described in Joel were pushed into mourning and sadness after learning that while the "drink and grain" offerings were being withheld, there was nothing they could do to appease God or attract His presence to the sacrifices.

This sadness carries on for us in the church age when pastors realize how the "grain and drink" offerings are being withheld. This is evidenced in the prevailing presence of the spirit of entertainment instead of the spirit of holiness, and the drive for material blessings instead of the pursuit of Christlike mindedness. Pastors and leaders everywhere should be driven into mourning and sadness when they realized that what should be a celebration of Christ at our services is lacking the intimate and sincere remembrance of what Christ has done and has been replaced with a desire to come to church just to get something from God. Sadly, instead of mourning, many ministries hire exciting worship teams and robust technology in hopes of creating, through flashy shows, what will no longer manifest with the simplicity of hearts seeking after God's presence.

4. Joel 1:14 – *"Announce a sacred fast; proclaim a solemn assembly! Gather the elders and all the residents of the land at the house of the LORD your God, and cry out to the LORD."* If we reach this point and nothing we can do will attract the presence of God

to us, what do we do? We go to him, the right way.

"Announce a sacred fast." Who was supposed to fast? The context of this verse implies that **everyone** was to be invited to fast. Not just the elders and the leaders. Now, I've not been to every prayer event on the planet, but I have yet to attend one where the invitation to fast for the people or community was passed beyond the initial planning group, leaders, or church members. A perfect example of what it looks like when everyone is invited to fast and pray is in Joel 2:15–17 (emphasis added):

> *Blow the ram's horn in Zion! Announce a sacred fast; proclaim a solemn assembly.* Gather the people; *sanctify the congregation;* assemble the aged; gather the infants, even babies nursing at the breast. Let the groom leave his bedroom, and the bride her honeymoon chamber. *Let the priests, the* LORD*'s ministers, weep between the portico and the altar. Let them say: "Have pity on your people,* LORD*, and do not make your inheritance a disgrace, an object of scorn among the nations. Why should it be said among the peoples, 'Where is their God?'"*

"Call a solemn assembly, gather the elders and all the inhabitants of the land into the house of the LORD" (Joel 1:14 KJV). According to the Oxford dictionary, a solemn assembly is something done in a solemn manner and is categorized by being formal, dignified, not done cheerfully or smiling but seriously and with deep sincerity. This can only be done if the seriousness of the matter is explained while inviting everyone to the fast, followed by an invitation to solemnly gather after the agreed fasting period. We must not make light of what is happening in our community; there is nothing to be jovial about given the fact that the diminished presence of God has allowed the enemy to run through our community. Let everyone fast together and solemnly gather.

"And cry out to the Lord"—as we gather solemnly and seriously, our goal is not to seek blessings, but to seek God Himself. We are crying out about the things happening in our community that are bringing about the day of the Lord.

As We Obey These Steps, a Promise Comes to Light

The steps God gives us through the words of Joel are not meant to be used as a "four-step program to the presence of God"; rather, they should be used as a guide for making our hearts right as we position ourselves at the throne of God and await His response as pictured in Joel 2:12–14:

> *Even now—this is the LORD's declaration—turn to me with all your heart, with fasting, weeping, and mourning. Tear your hearts, not just your clothes, and return to the LORD your God. For he is gracious and compassionate, slow to anger, abounding in faithful love, and he relents from sending disaster. Who knows? He may turn and relent and leave a blessing behind him, so you can offer a grain offering and a drink offering to the LORD your God.*

With that said, we do have an awesome promise that we can expect when our hearts are truly broken and repentant as we seek God's face in obedience with the instructions laid before us!

In Joel 2:18–27, everything that happens after the word *Then* in verse 18 is beautiful imagery of all that God is free to do out of His incomprehensible pool of grace and mercy. Below are a few notable actions from God taken from this passage:

- He begins to be jealous for us again (speaking of a love that a husband has for a bride).

- He begins to heal our land and economy till we are satisfied with all the increase!
- Verse 20 tells us that God will drive from us the enemies' armies that have decimated our community and territory.
- Verses 25–27 say that He will ultimately restore to our community and with it our purpose, which was lost while our territory was under bondage.

Please take a moment and read for yourself this wonderful passage and ask God to speak to you through it:

> *Then the* L*ORD* *became jealous for his land and spared his people. The* L*ORD* *answered his people: Look, I am about to send you grain, new wine, and fresh oil. You will be satiated with them, and I will no longer make you a disgrace among the nations.*
>
> *I will drive the northerner far from you and banish him to a dry and desolate land, his front ranks into the Dead Sea, and his rear guard into the Mediterranean Sea. His stench will rise; yes, his rotten smell will rise, for he has done astonishing things.*

Don't be afraid, land; rejoice and be glad, for the Lord *has done astonishing things.*

Don't be afraid, wild animals, for the wilderness pastures have turned green, the trees bear their fruit, and the fig tree and grapevine yield their riches. Children of Zion, rejoice and be glad in the Lord *your God, because he gives you the autumn rain for your vindication. He sends showers for you, both autumn and spring rain as before. The threshing floors will be full of grain, and the vats will overflow with new wine and fresh oil.*

I will repay you for the years that the swarming locust ate, the young locust, the destroying locust, and the devouring locust—my great army that I sent against you. You will have plenty to eat and be satisfied. You will praise the name of the Lord *your God, who has dealt wondrously with you. My people will never again be put to shame. You will know that I am present in Israel and that I am the* Lord *your God, and there is no other. My people will never again be put to shame.*

—Joel 2:18–27

How You Can Bring Deliverance to Your Community?

As urgent and important as it is to serve as a catalyst to bring deliverance to your community, the best word of advice I can give you to begin your journey is this: "Start slow; then move fast."

That's right, start slow. First understand that by moving too fast in your zeal to bring repentance and revival, you can actually "do" what God wants, but not the "way" that He said to do it. And no good thing can be done a wrong way and still be considered good. Let's look at the example from Ezra 9 and 10.

In chapter 9 Ezra discovers through the reports of the princes that the people are in sin, and that the leaders were responsible for the great sin entering into the community. Instead of rushing in to challenge the people and call them to repentance, Ezra goes into mourning, fasting, praying, and intercession over the people, asking God to show grace. He did this because the people could not stand before God in their current state of national sin. Only after this, in the first six verses of chapter 10, do we get to see what Ezra does to catalyze the people into confession and repentance. In other words, he started slowly by going to God to acknowledge the sins of the people and asking for God's grace and mercy. Then after having spoken to God and obtained mercy, he moved very quickly in his actions with the people serving as a catalyst to bring about national confession and repentance. Because Ezra started slowly and acted toward God first, a "large assembly" gathered around him and were brought into conviction, confession, and repentance so that he was allowed to move quickly, as the people asked him to "Be strong and take action!"

Read Ezra 9 and 10 and you'll see that all the steps from Joel that we reviewed above are taking place here also. The main thing I want you to see is that Ezra's strategy of how to get out of sin, "putting away the strange wives," came only after all the steps involved with coming to God were completed.

For your community and mine, we must have faith that if we follow the steps we have learned about here, God will give us the strategy to get our communities out of sin. For Ezra and some of the other Jewish leaders, it was an 88-day plan to properly come out of sin. What will it take for our communities? For every sin problem there is a strategy to overcome—it doesn't matter what the situation is! But we mustn't move ahead of God. Allow Him to give you the plan after you and then the community come to Him in repentance. Then, and only then, move fast to accomplish the plan as God has detailed it to you.

Trust God to speak to you about who to involve with you during the slow part of coming to God. Remember, you are not alone in sensing God wanting to bring repentance and revival to your community. Ezra worked with other leaders to accomplish the goal; you will need to also. Trust God to lead you to them and discern who is not in your best interest to trust.

Reflections

CLOSING: FINAL WORDS

Be encouraged: community deliverance has happened before; it will happen again. In Ezra 9–10 we see a great example of a community being set free from sin and delivered from bondage. All the essential elements were there that would lead a community to go into bondage and territorial oppression. There was great sin among the people of God with those in leadership being the main perpetrators of the sin. A foreign force was allowed to subdue the territory and the people because of the sins of the nation, which over the years had turned into generational sin. By God's grace this story also includes all that is needed to attract the presence of God and bring freedom to the people and region. The people who alerted

Ezra knew that there was a sin problem in the land and alerted Ezra, who went into great mourning and prayer.

Notice how everyone who trembled at the words of God gathered to pray and repent with Ezra. We are given neither their age nor status, only that anyone who feared the Word of the Lord was there to pray and repent. The request from the people was that God would deliver them from sin, bondage, and oppression during the "brief moment of grace" that was afforded to them. Ezra led the assembly of men, women, and children through sincere prayer and repentance; as he did so, a strategy for freedom and deliverance was revealed to them. The plan took 88 days from start (Ezra 10:9) to finish (Ezra 10:17) before the people and the land were free.

It is my prayer that you ask God for a "brief moment of grace" for your community and that during that time the people's hearts would turn to God in sincere repentance. Who knows, God just may turn and relent and leave a blessing behind (Joel 2:14).

ABOUT THE AUTHOR

Having been called to faith in Christ at the tender age of six years old, Parris dreamed he would be a pastor one day. That dream fueled a passion in him that led him to establish Agape Community Bible Church in late June 2009. Having been born in the small military town of Fort Polk near Leesville, Louisiana, Parris grew in the knowledge of God's Word, being trained by his father, who had led his first congregation there.

Shortly after attending the University of Houston, Pastor Parris was called to serve as an associate minister of Liberty Baptist Church, where he periodically preached Sunday messages and led church-sponsored marriage and financial conferences.

At his father's request in 2002, Parris agreed to join him on staff at Charis Chapel Bible Church, where Parris also attended Charis Theological Seminary and received his master of theology in 2006. That same year, upon his ordination, he was invited to serve as youth pastor at Charis Bible Church while also serving as a professor of apologetics in the seminary. At the age of 31, having served in those roles for two years, he began to be overwhelmingly convicted that the time was ripe for him to fulfill God's call on his life to pastor his own congregation. Three years earlier, God's vision had launched him forward to file paperwork to establish what is currently the Agape Community Bible Church.

In faith, he began holding Bible studies in his home on Wednesday evenings. Shortly thereafter, he secured the gym at Arizona Fleming Elementary School and on June 28, 2009, the very first worship service was held. Agape Community Bible Church looks forward to showing love to the body of Christ by reaching out to her community, evangelizing the city through the application of God's Word, and sharing the values of "Family, Edification, and Doctrinal Sanctification."

NOTES

1. *New Encyclopedia Britannica*, s.v. "Tammuz," Vol. 1, 532.
2. "Atheism Doubles Among Generation Z," January 24, 2018, https://www.barna.com/research/atheism-doubles-among-generation-z/.
3. Ibid.
4. "Most Twentysomethings Put Christianity on the Shelf Following Spiritually Active Teen Years," September 11, 2006, https://www.barna.com/research/most-twenty-somethings-put-Christianity-on-the-shelf-following-spiritually-active-teen-years/.
5. Ibid.

www.ingramcontent.com/pod-product-compliance
Lightning Source LLC
Chambersburg PA
CBHW051430090426
42737CB00014B/2906

* 9 7 8 1 9 5 3 3 0 0 8 4 3 *